a
suburb of Belsen

The poetry of
STANLEY ROGER GREEN

with drawings by
GEOFFREY ROPER

Paul Harris Publishing, Edinburgh

First published 1977 by
PAUL HARRIS PUBLISHING,
25 London Street, Edinburgh.

ISBN 0 904505 21 9 (cased)
ISBN 0 904505 22 7 (paper)

Published with the assistance of the Scottish Arts Council.

Printed in Scotland by the Shetland Times Ltd.,
Lerwick, Shetland.

STANLEY ROGER GREEN was educated by the skylines of Edinburgh, the hills and wildwoods of Clackmannanshire, the ports and seaboards of the world, and a few sporadic teachers.

A poet, artist, musician and composer, he has sold paintings, played in orchestras and written chamber music. He was the winner of the Henry Mair Scottish Open Poetry Award in 1975. As an architect his works have been awarded three honourable mentions by the Saltire Society and he has designed and built the upgraded villages of Balerno and Kirknewton. His poetry, plays and short stories have been broadcast by the BBC and widely published in magazines, although this is his first collection to be published in book form.

Related to Robert Burns, he shares with Scotland's immortal bard a discernment for small creatures in the universal context and love features large, although sometimes painfully.

Stanley Green's first poems were composed at the helm of a tramp steamer while crossing the Indian Ocean (the poet had sailed around the world at the age of nineteen). These are not the poems of an ivory-towered intellectual: "Poetry to me is, at once, a compulsive method of transmuting the raw ore of experience into art, and a means of establishing nodal points of order in a crowded life."

GEOFFREY ROPER is a professional artist who lives and works in Edinburgh. He has had nineteen one-man shows in London, Edinburgh, Dublin, Harrogate and Middlesborough. He exhibits regularly with the Fine Art Society in London and Edinburgh and has achieved a very considerable reputation as one of Scotland's leading artists. The drawings for this book were specially commissioned.

CONTENTS

ANIMALS

Caterpillar

Treading by the stream
I almost crushed it underfoot
Dressed for a football match
Playing concertinas with itself

With the arrogance of giantism
I laid it on my palm
The softest movement
Like a nudge from a moth

And it had curled into
A furry Catherine-wheel
Pretending to be
Somewhere else

But tracing the stream's light
Down the corrie to the loch
Below hills serrating
A sky flecked with hawks

I knew it to be there
At the centre of a world
I had stumbled into
Making mine briefly whole

Rain whispered in the bracken
I made a warm tent of my hands
With a chancel window
To look inside

Take Care Little Rabbit

We heard the bell of hounds
On the hill's far side
Saw them flushing bracken
And they weren't looking
For tennis balls

We, that is, daughter perched
On a crag gazing seawards
And self, awaiting thought's return
Turned as the hounds
Rolled silence up the scree

We dodged round a cliff
To escape splinters
From the shattered afternoon
And there we saw you
Transfixed in profile

Like an old cameo
An alert eye of agate.
Winter sunlight
Netted the corrie
Snared us all in gold

You and she dressed
Sensibly for winter
In rabbit skins, and self
Making do with the coat
Of my dead brother

Take care little rabbit
Oh take care

Philosophers

In Rosslyn Glen wild hyacinth
Stand like toytown soldiers
A platoon of blue alertness
Awaiting orders to march

Strutting pheasants appear
To review the ranks
Of bell helmets, leaf spears
But not like puffing majors

More they resemble
Donnish philosophers
Coat-tails thrust out
Eyes Earthbound

Pecking at this man's truth
Chopping at that man's logic
Nodding at intervals
In peripatetic debate

A dog barks, at once
They abandon theses
And the ranks of hyacinth
And fly cackling to safety

To extol the correctness
Of their action and review
Their clear position from the lowest
Rungs of a tree's leafy ladder

Reluctant Knight

Seen from the road across the bald meadow
The clump of trees, dense and breathing
Beechwood, copper beech, bottle-green cedars
Looked more animal than vegetable
A primeval shape, a leafy saurian
A dragon drowsing in summer haze
Snapping at stray birds

It had bitten off a lane otherwise
You would never guess it had once
Devoured a house but not quite whole
In autumn for instance when veils

Of leaves fall you may discern
A dormer window blinking at daylight
A porch stifling a yawn and a scaly
Tower like a thrusting horn above
A belvedere so that you cannot tell

Which is predator and which
The half-digested prey

In winter when raw winds flay its lair
Red anger flares from windows
A half-seen gateway bares its teeth
And hot smoke snorts from chimneys
Folk pass by on tiptoe then

Is there a thethered maiden in there
Awaiting deliverance from durance vile?

She could wait long enough for me

Once I saw a sheep trot up the lane
I waited but it never came out again

It's Conservation Year

Quick, said my love, under the hawthorns
under the moon and stars without number
Quickly, said she, ready to crush me
then I noticed a hedgehog starting to lumber

Over the lawn and glinting with dew
trundling along as though still in slumber
Now, said the girl, a rose opening to gather
me into her petals, My dear, I would rather

Just examine this hedgehog with its black
brilliant eye and fresh dew on its back
Now, said my love, and embraced me entire-
ly, under the hawthorns, leaves rimmed with fire

Off went the hedgehog on his grub-picking way
a prickly haggis, a pin-cushion tank
Goodbye Erinaceous, I'll return some day
and search the woods and the flowering bank

Or wait under the hawthorns and stars without number
for my pin-cushion friend to suddenly lumber
Over the lawn with fresh dew on his back
a tongue of quicksilver and his eye brilliant black

LOVE

Hippomenes and the Ratrace

In the canteen's clattering din
And self-service bustle I see you
And my mind blows out like a gasket
As you park your tray near mine
Their plastic lips just touching
Beside my briefcase as usual

Would I pass the salt? you ask
Unaware that I would pass
The escarpments of Karakorum
At a nod from your midnight brows

I grant your thin request and wish
For crystals of a richer light
Diamonds brighter than Arcturus
Sapphires more blue than Bermudian reefs

Busy to day! you say, Always is
Day before wages. Just listen
To the invoice department!

I gaze through a veil of golden
Stars and see my phantom
Colleagues enveloping
The shepherds pie and hear
Beyond the dutiful munch
Of clerical mandibles
My heart burst open
With inner voices
Of sunlit waterfalls
And singing birds of paradise

See you! you say, by way
Of valediction and plunge back
Into the typing pool
Leaving a desert in the clattering
Room and soon the greasy dishes
Will be cleared from round
The oasis of this poem

B

Spurs should come out on top, Saturday!
Shouts Bunshaw watching me scribble
That's more than I will, I think
Seeing the moon fall behind
The ivoried temples of whispering Atlantis
As I slip the remains of her applecore
Into my briefcase as usual

Peevish Woman

You occupied the royal suite of my soul
And complained of draughts
You held the keys to all my doors
And let them rust
You had a ringside seat at all my contests
And kept throwing in towels

You watched my dramas from the wings
I couldn't hear the prompter for your catcalls
The tears that arose to obscure the scene
Were too salty, they would spoil your make-up
You viewed my universe from a planetarium
And thought the constellations ungainly

Together we rehearsed the music of the spheres
But you required a descant from others
The ripening diapason which engulfs
The sunset splendour which unites
Filled you with fear of harmony and the dark
You switched on raucous artificial noons

Lady, you would ascend the staircase of heaven
And find cobwebs at every baluster
The robes and coiffures of the seraphim
You would think hopelessly out of fashion
And you would look around Creation and declare
That God had delusions of grandeur

Poem

If a moon had sailed above the town
That night I could have borne her leaving
Better, seen her walk away in silver
Not then grieving, heard her shoes

On the stoney pavement kick up echoes
Watched her dwindle into distance
Merge with silence and the past
A stone in a pool both stilled at last

But it was raining when the door
Slammed shut behind her: for a moment
The rush of wind and rain filled
Our space where no words were spoken

Only a blurred shape glimpsed through
The window, and the glass pane
Streaming with endless tears as though
It was the night whose heart was broken

Incubus

Yesterday I awoke a free man
Finding her dead within me
So without waiting for darkness
Orisons or drumrolls
I wrapped her in a shroud of regrets
And tipped her over my raillery

Into a sea of forgetfulness
Where she sank leaving not even
A bubble of champagne behind her
I invited both of her friends to the wake
And later she telephoned demanding
To know what I was playing at

Showing no respect for the feelings
Of the bereaved was typical of her
So I cut short the mourning
And hauled my flag to the masthead again
Informing her that I was not a medium
The dead could carry their own messages

It was not the kind of communication
That Graham Bell had in mind
When he invented the instrument, I said
Today I met her in the street
Looking as fresh and substantial
As only someone can who means nothing to you

She spoke some words to which
I made no reply and passed on
For it is unlucky to converse with the dead
Just look at what happened to Hamlet
Tomorrow though is the third day
It would be like her to imitate Christ

Next Spring

She wept as our past was dismantled
Stitch by stitch, unthreading seams
For long invisible, placing in groups
The parts, hers, mine, the uncertain 'ours'

Outside the garden filled with rain
Laburnums and rowans drooped
Their mist of whitening buds seeming
Tactless, arrived in the wrong season

Yet a pair of blackbirds were busy
Amiably bickering by the rubble wall
Ruffling the bunched ivy they used each year
We would not witness home-making next spring

The children would not clamber jostling
Up the ladder to check progress
On the clutch of straining beaks
And cataracted eyes next spring

A garden fork and a hoe leaned
Expectantly on a fence. I had planned
A rosebed and a row of beeches
The weeping pulsed on through emptying rooms

Apparation

The warm day still as a tomb
Clouds pierced quivering
On treetops like spiked notes
With no replies expected

Threshers combed the barley
With spumes of dusty silence
Then a bird dropped darkly under
The boughs and the sudden sun

Illumining the falling movement
Struck snow-in-summer
Beneath neglected roses
A blow of glancing gold

And it seemed that hovering
On insect-thrumming air
A shadow of your living form
Hung frozen between moment

And moment and whitened
Above the dazzling lawn
And darker foliage beyond
Your almost self then vanished

With my startled impossible
Greeting arrested on my lips
And a flower halfway to yours
Or was it a faint gesture

Of farewell, of renunciation
For the sunlight that retreated
For darkness I could not lighten
For burdens I did not share

The bird swooped up again
And the deserted garden
Resumed its purpose with
The intricate business of summer

Then guests arrived from Oxford
For afternoon tea on the lawn
Sunlight and drowsy laughter
The rich flash of living eyes

Love Country

I know the landscape well
Swamps pitted with blunders
Cliff edges ribbed with clinging
Worn smooth with sudden descents
I can taste like the afterglow
Of old wine the intricate flavour
Of imminent ambush

No use warning others of hazards
All landscapes appear different
Though pitfalls and snares are the same
Yet bruised and scarred I can
Still make a new journey
And be surprised by it all
All over again

One could always avoid the journey
Sit quiet as in a picture gallery
And learn how others saw the world
Safe from storms, the frosts, the blinding heat
With no prowling menace leaping
From the forest ready to rend
Your heart into shreds of grief

PEOPLE

Helen

Her beauty strikes like lightning or roses
Save that it's a miracle if you breathe unscathed
At her approach tears break out from
The adamant heart as if smote by a rod of Moses

Even the dust at her feet chassés in air
Into dancing geometry of Circassian circles
Even the clouds soar into anthems
Above the rostrum of her hair

Sometimes I'm invisible to her
But on certain days she will smile
From her immeasurable distance as though I were
The horizon assuming a familiar contour

So that she may arrest my trance
With that slow exquisite gesture
She has perfected so humanely
To ease the intolerable wound of her glance

When goals recede men will twist in vain
To gaze from their gyves on her beauty aware
That in the unspent furnace of desire
Another Troy could burn again

Other bugles rouse captains from wine, call
Princes from court, unleash the pennoned fleets
To sparkle plains with fires of new myrmidons
To settle another Olympian brawl

She would smile and bow delicately with that slow
Gesture she has perfected to ease the wound
Of her glance, while a city perished in flame
And the spores of fable fell round her like snow

Small Ad

Lost
A gay dog about town
Wearing a downturned smile
And a winter coat of stale
Emotions turned inside out
To conceal a threadbare purpose

Friendly to strangers
Who might be of use
Fond of children
For whole minutes at a time
Eats anything
At the best restaurants
Drinks gin and French mainly
Answers to Old Chap
When bluff is called
Good with horses
But snaps at tips
That go unplaced

Last seen wandering
Between the cocktail bars
And the wrong bedrooms
In search of a new gloss
To an old coat grown shaggy
With rubbing shoulders
Against the right people
For reasons he can't remember

No reward to finder

Just try keeping him

The Tramp

Do you see that tramp
On the wayside bench
That commemorates a forgotten baillie?

Yes, him with the sou-wester
Laid on his chest
Like a last-year's wreath

Most folk pass him by
Not me, for that's how
He loses heart and lets himself go

Give him a coin
And a fag and that
Will restore his flickering faith

See how it combs out
His unspeakable face
With a new herring-bone dignity

Lights a remote
Candle in the crazed
Depths of his snailhead eyes

Watch him step out
To dine now
Down to the red-biddy shop

To discuss the world
With his peers
See him go flicking out

His sou-wester
Like an opera hat
Shuffling downhill with rheumatic aplomb

For he has cheated
The law and the worms
And laboratories for another day

'Well now' he seems
To tell the sky
'You've made a mess of things, haven't you?'

'But nobody's perfect,
There's no hard feelings'
And off he goes absolving God of everything

But he never
Absolves me
Never absolves me of anything

Theme and Variations

I

Before he had started shaving
He left his schoolmates
Except for Danny who went with him
And signed on at the pit
They gave him a helmet and shovel
And told him to get busy
He hated it but there seemed little choice at the time

II

At nineteen he married pregnant Annie
It could have been anyone's
Except for Danny who was best man
But he signed on at the registrar's
They gave him a council house and a stony garden
His wife handed him a pick and shovel
Showed him what she wanted done
And told him to get busy
He hated it but there seemed little choice at the time

III

War interrupted the tedium
All his workmates remained down the pit
Except for Danny so they went together
And signed on with the Sappers
They gave him a uniform and a badge
The sergeant handed him a pick and shovel
And told him to get busy
Showed him how trenches were dug
He hated it but there seemed little choice at the time

IV

At Hal-Fayah Rommel pasted them
His unit was almost wiped out
Except for Danny who fell later
And signed on with Death
A scrap of shrapnel sticking from his eye

33

C

A surviving corporal handed him a pick and shovel
Showed him how the dead were buried
And told him to get busy
He hated it but there seemed little choice at the time

V

Back in civvy street he bought some greyhounds
And trained them between the slagheaps
Where Danny used to train his greyhounds
And signed on at the burroo
They offered him jobs which he turned down
The clerk handed him forms and cards
Showed him how to fill them up
And told him to get busy
But a lesson had been learned; he was never busy again

The Bigots

When he was two years old
The country of his mind
Was imperceptiby invaded
For you're never too young
To learn, opined his mentors

And over the years the scars
Of skirmishes and forays
Began to furrow his face
Crumpling the features
Into furtive knots of
Preoccupied territory

He kept a cross above the hearth
And a portrait of Christ's mother
Eyes upturned as though expecting rain
And exposing a blood-curdling organ
Unknown to medical science
Behind her neatly forcipated breast

Looking through rimless
Rosary-coloured spectacles
He saw a pit blackening
Beneath me and a gallows
Sprouting from the top of my head
Over his hovered a white dove
And a choir of bats from
The chapel belfry

Propped on his crutch of faith
He reminds me of
A tame Long John Silver
With a patch of theology
Obscuring half his vision

And just look at that
Holy ghost of a parrot
Preening and leering
Over his shoulder

SOCIETY

'If You Want To Find His Monument'

Look at that building
You may find it hard to believe
But it was my idea
From conception to parturition
Now they're going to take me inside

Soon I must pass under the arcuate lintol
An innovation copied now everywhere
And enter those rounded walls
Strong to keep time and weather out
Not me, you'd think, the creator, in

They're coming for me now
Soon I must cross that threshold
Note the cunning way it has been
Merged into the plinth course
So that it seems to grow from the earth

I know the little room
Where I'll go for the questioning
The clerestory window
Too high to escape from
Soundproofed so no-one will hear cries

I designed it like a private chapel
No-one will hear prayers either
No projections anywhere
From which to hang yourself afterwards
If there is an afterwards

It was written of Wren
In the nave of St Paul's
'If you want to find his monument
Look around you'
Once inside my magnum opus I'll be nameless

When you come to plan your life
Make sure that you're not designing
A mausoleum, for if you did
It would be no-one else's miscalculation
And you can't go back to the drawing board

Figureheads

A Nemadi from Saharan wastes
Or Bushman from the Kalahari
Blundering on a treeless shore
And viewing the improbable aspect
Of a ship bearing its intricate
Load of cross-rigged spears
And captive clouds of sail
Float over an endless lake
Devoid of other boundaries
Would fall down amazed
And cry to monstrous deities
For explanation or atonement

Then he might at last
Behold the figurehead
And believe in his primitive
Fashion that this gaudy
Outstretched talisman
Was the motive force
That made the vessel move
Obeying her silent commands
And cleaving the purple silk
Of the waters into glittering disarray
For her inscrutable pleasure
As she stares with corpse-bright
Sightless eyes at the empty horizon
Smiling with lunatic radiance

Cultures

In a garden near Vancouver
Placed more for effect than ceremony
A totem pole broods over
Ogling Caucasians, tourist and lover
Camera film from the log-cabin shop
Snaps up its awesome length non-stop

Carved over centuries
With motifs and grotesqueries
Anthropoid brutes, bestial heads
And a turtle naturally
Old symbol of longevity
All painted in authentic shades

For it is politic now at last
To preserve the culture of the past
Across the natural harbour straits
In the mountain's shadow in stealth
The Indian squats in poverty
On envied lands of freehold wealth

They get drunk without ceremony
Wait for death from imported bacilli
They show no gratitude these squatters
For the right to fish in polluted waters
Sequestered by cedar and maple
And crowns of the tumbling sequoia

They cannot see from that far shore
Their ancient tribal totem pole
They have no wampum for the ferry shuttle
Nor heart for an empty pilgrimage
Since their gods have deserted them
Or have been vanquished in mystic battle

Across the harbour straits each day
They see Caucasian towers rise
Taller totems of conquering deities
Blue Shield, Sears Roebuck, Coca-Cola
And a Hilton naturally
New symbol of ubiquity

Indians are not made welcome
At the new victorious totems
Officials would turn them away
Without ceremony or sanction
For it is politic now and decent
To protect the culture of the present

CITY

Puritan Town

I saw a naked cloud last night
A cumulo-nimbus by Rubens
A voyeur moon leered
Behind laced cirrus curtains

Blue shadows were cast on misty
Thighs and nebulous breasts
And that boudoir airborne Venus
Drifted over my puritan town

Upright with towers and steeples
And one-legged builders' cranes
Somewhere a siren wailed
Car doors thudded shut

Pubs exhuded anguished fumes
Gaunt roofs threw up chimney stacks
In attitudes of frozen outrage
Tall windows glowered down

Each one a mirror
To the Venus cloud
Admiring its reclining image
Before melting into

The flagrant arms of the moon
And all the clocks of my
Puritan town struck the hour
In peels of desperate dismay

News Flash

The children poke the screen like a fire
to evoke flickering faces from the ether
to fill the yawning void
between supper and bedtime

Half a world away a broken army
spills from a jungle leaving villages
in cinders, pot-bellied children spotted
with yaws, unblinking at cameras and fate
tattered soldiery climb rungs of dead
comrades to crowded decks, rifle-butted

Women fall back in the bloodbath harbour
bombs scream, planes zoom
a ship of refugees explodes
a state has toppled, a culture
has been utterly destroyed
the children sip cocoa, read comic strips

Then with no scheduled announcement a pacifist
blackbird repeats a morsed note of grief
from a shaking bough in the panic-filled
garden where a frantic mate searches wildly
for tailless younglings cat-scattered
another springtime's programme interrupted

The children leave the screen at once
find younglings, feed them warm milk
chopped worms and crumbs of cake
tend them for days, eschew all games
to lend them strength to fly upwards
for the first singing lesson

We hear at last shrill notes
and normal service is resumed
the children poke the screen like a fire
to evoke flickering faces from the ether
to fill the yawning void
between supper and bedtime

A Suburb of Belsen

Somewhere in the rear gardens of our terrace
With baffled squeals and nagging plaintive howls
A tethered hound is forever complaining

The geranium grower pottering in the shed
The stolid gardener clumping round the compost
The contemplative admiring the slow reversion of roses

All are now accustomed to the dismal barking
Behind the laburnums its regularity is accepted
Like the nuisance of weeds or the marmalade tomcat

Who impregnates the children's tabbies
With enviable rapacity, or like frost
Or the man down the street who is said to drink

But my neighbour over the ivied wall
Sometimes confesses to a wry discomfort
'Something should be done about that dog'

He says, 'It lowers the tone of the place'
He would rather it was taken away or put down
As though captivity was like a distemper

Blandly he ignores the ferocious concrete
Erection beyond the tennis courts
And blames the urban drains for the faint
Acrid whiff of withering flesh

A View from Calton Hill

An ice age glacier carved this footstool
To crag and tail formation, pimpled now
With small observatories squinting
Through sodium-stained night skies
I look the other way, observe the town

There stood the house where Robert Burns
Over a dish of tea paid illicit court
To Clarinda, such genteel perfidy
And he to romp and carouse with scullions
Later in the noisome howffs of Canongate

Below a highway roars where once
The whores silently bawled their wares
Pimps flickered darkly, drunk seamen
Fought in the polyglot street and the Law
Looked on bemused as keepers in a zoo

Across the chasm where a Georgian square
Was toppled, once shabby but dignified
Like a bereft duchess down on her luck
A lump of hound-patrolled Chicago
Now blocks a view of hills and home

Tower blocks gather on city fringes
Wait till numbers increase before advancing
Already their spies the cranes have alighted
Are selecting morsels of the living town
We are taught not to complain of progress

And behind those towers loom shadows
Are they the shadows of unbuilt towers
Rank upon rank of them advancing
Like a wall, a tidal wave of shadows
Is it the Ice again, so soon?

Botanic Garden

Beneath the willows by the pool
Old leaves and new lovers entwine
Silhouette against a world full of compromise
And an empty skyblue future pierced
By a steeple above the warehouse nave
Waiting for countdown to uncertain regions

Galleon swans and duck flotillas
Ignore the gulls weary of drumming
The lawns for gullible worms
They cry and somersault on the wind
That sprays invisible crumbs
On the pool's pale mirror

I stand interpolating chance
And throw my crumbs of contact
To all the birds and lovers
Of next year's springtime
An imperfect system with imbalanced
Tables. *Rien ne va plus*

The American oak, the Chinese larch
And the Russian sycamore nod their
Winter heads with sycophantic
Agreement to the wind's reasoning
Fallen leaves crumble and mutter
Under the boughs their protest stilled

The lovers move on and more leaves fall
The wind drops its argument and silently
The trees gather their robes
About them like despairing diplomats
Abandoned by a coup d'etat
Irrelevant in an alien land

49

HOMELAND

Skotia

A form of the word means darkness
In the tongue of ancient Greece

Some say a princess of Pharaoh's Egypt
For reasons as veiled as her beauty

Reigned as queen of pagan Munster
And sailed for purposes of state

To Caledon's promontories
And bequeathed her royal name

On the misty crags and forests
We now call homeland

I think a moping centurion
On guard duty from Corstopitum

Treading that serpentine wall
Anxious about another breach

Made at the latest skirmish
By the heedless Selgovae

Drenched by Border rainfall
Chilled by the nagging wind

Suddenly remembered
The wine and the cypresses

High noon on the Appian Way
Sunlit panoplies in the Fora Romanum

The slaves and the carnivals
The circus and the triumphs

The mad blues and frantic greens
In the tumult of the Hippodrome

I think he wrapped his cloak
Tighter about him and peered

Northwards into gathering mirk
Skotia, he said, recalling

A classical education
Skotia, he said

This Garden Now

This garden now advises flight
Here great cats growl and wheel about
The thorns devour the roses light
But what it might be like without
Our zeal and tireless guard, I guess
A deserted swamp or wilderness

This neat but ample ice-capped sphere
With matronly waist of torrid zones
May try our animal strength it's clear
But what it might be like without
Our zeal and tireless guard, I doubt
A charnel house of shattered bones

This firmament some try to flout
May be policed to finite ends
By quantum maths and tinpot stigmas
But what it might be like without
Our zeal and tireless guard, my friends
An infinite sea of twinkling enigmas

This able hand I place in yours
May drop its burden now with pleasure
This questing eye transfixing yours
Desist its vigil but just for the present
Without these tools to make the ascent
What would our love use then for measure

Spent minds relieved of modern cramps
And set adrift would in a while
Reach reptile-threaded mangrove swamps
Where stars wink out and cease to hover
Like snuffed candles, the long feast over
Where the sun's mirth fades to a lunar smile

Bavelaw in Winter

Searching late for a Bronze Age cairn
I saw the reservoir glittering through
A row of blackened pinewood: it formed
A cretin's gaptoothed grin through which
Cold winds drew breath for bleak syllables
On the subject of desolation
Pewter clouds raced over skull-shaped
Hills and mangled what was left of sky

Place and time felt warped out of focus
The city behind me hid under its own
Miasma like a threatened squid
And it seemed the peat-hag riddled moor
Could sprout a herd of mastodon
Almost I saw them troop across Golgotha
And heard instead of burbling curlew
A pterodactyl tear the wind to shreads

And rearing huge in the bloodshot eye
Of the sun tyrannosaurus rex
Grappling with annihilation
Where druids flared up antique festivals
And now asthmatic sheep turn up collars
Against the winds of night,
I turn up mine and head for home
A Bronze Age cairn will keep till spring

Kirk of Glencorse

Within a mile of Rullion Green
Sharp incense of wild garlic pierces
Like the carillon of throstles rising
In a cloister of trees as solemn as elders

Only a shell remains, as old as the Covenant
And a squat steeple shorn of slates
No bell within and windhewn clouds
Vault over a bare transepted nave

A wind sotto voice in the organ loft
A hoodie-crow carping a sermon
To congregations of nodding ferns
And comatose headstones in uncut grass

The weathered rubrics cryptic now
As baffling as Chaldean hieroglyphs
Beneath 'Their name liveth for evermore'
The windworn record of a farmer's ilk

It seemed that consecration had leaked
Away through gaps in time and masonry
Then a cloud burst open like a miser's purse
Gilding the air with sudden benediction

SEACALL

Safe Anchorage

The ship storm-battered
Lifeboats and awning spars gone
Rigging frosted with salt
Sulks like a child
Limps home to rest
Like a beaten dog

Finally anchored in the bay
Familiar woods above the town
Sheltering hills beyond
Known figures wandering
The quayside throwing
Handlines and welcomes

Yet the storm loaned purpose
Pared gestures to essentials
As an artist might do
Honed the blade of life
To a fine cutting edge
Ready for swift conflict

In this safe anchorage
Barnacles and weeds clutch
The hull seductively
Heath winds beguile us
And rust, silent mischief
Spreads a net of slow decay

Unofficial Log Entry

Thirty days eastward sailing from Durban
And we berthed for coal at Wallaroo
Where dusk falls flat with scattered glints
Like stage scenery or a sandbag cosh,
Macnab went thirsting for half-caste bints

Dusky as nuts they came and as pungent
As sweet smoke up the downwind road
Rolling and laughing like waves on the Bight
And the boozers were shutting at six of the clock
And the mad gulls flapped in the last of the light

Wallaroo shook out crumpled bats to dry
From under the milk bars' awnings
The Southern Cross was a silver wreath
Pinned high on the coffin nightsky
Verandahs grinned down with rusting teeth

Macnab split the bosun's scalp like a mango
In a friendly game of poker for bints
Who sang mission hymns as we played or snored
Then we drank the rotgut plonk till dawn
And sailed with the tide none sober aboard

MENACE

Armada

He stood out from the field
Like a gnarled tree
Stunned with years
And forgotten gales

And gazed his fill
While the sun's noon flail
Threshed swathes of light
On the sea's bright bowl

From the headland's height
He watched wings of cliff
Soar round the arc
Of silver surf
And dissolve in silence

Then under a branch
Of a fist for shade
And awed by a sudden
Gesture of peril
He saw the sea's rim flood
With distant sails

The progress of plague
Was not more resolute
Than the crescent menace
That stained the sea that day
And blood-drenched years
Sped aft beyond time's rim
To the birth of war
In the name of Christ
The Prince of Peace

Turning again to the
Questing hoe that seemed
To counterpoise
A natural symmetry

E

He worked with irreverent calm
His fathers' land
And let the worlds collide
Behind him with the
Mere clash of history

Missiles

Careless of fate
And aware of no destiny
Manannan Maclir
The dawn thunderer
Hurled megaliths
From the isle that takes his name
To abase the pride of Alba
And the Stone of Manau
Pierced the green heart
     Of Clackmanan

A more recent breast-beater
Threw growling bombers
From the plains of the Rhineland
Moonlit waves of them
Splashed through the clouds
     Of Clackmanan

Children of the storm
Are nowhere safe,
When gods play at war
Authority sardined us in trains
Sent them searching
For the quiet glen
The hidden village
Till we jolted to rest
Under a megalith's shadow
     In Clackmanan

The Stone of Manau
Became my lodestar
Its crude prism a pivot
To all my journeys
Past and future were hyphenated
By its unearthly silence
Between the high wall of hills
And the coiling rivers
     Of Clackmanan

Now I consider that megalith
Its black snout probing
The tall skies of Alba
Where diamond glints of warplanes
Hang poised in their traces
Playing tag with high mackerel
Aware of no destiny
And careless of fate

The Invaders

For half a thousand years or more
Old Stobo's tower had withstood sieges
Even ours, as children, were repulsed by fear
Of dusk that hung around the ramparts
Like folded wings of monstrous bats
And by day Stobo himself, a sombre
Hunchback whose life was a lone flag
Waved in battle as he hirpled towards
Our raiding party from the nearby thatched
And lightless hovel that was his home

The blackened turf crept through the gaping
Doorway where none but he dared enter
Except for beasts from the croft or wildwood
Rabbits and pigs, some balletic geese
That trumpeted like himself at our
Approach to his senile orchard or the maze
Of giant gooseberries; even small birds
Strutted indoors without a glance
At Stobo who we guessed maintained
Some dire and arcane pact with nature

Now Stobo is dead and buried somewhere
The tower's huge ashlar blocks of stone
Are cleaned of lichen and mortar-pointed
The broken crenellations reinstated
To withstand assaults from roving bands
Of tourists or earnest research students
Who sketch the slated cone on the turnpike
Staircase roof rebuilt by a department
For ancient monuments which prints a brochure
Of potted history and period plans

At weekends a computer consultant rents
Old Stobo's renovated cottage where concrete
Pantiles replace the sodden thatch
And painted harling hides the cracks

And moss, the doors and windows are trimmed
With varnished redwood frames by courtesy
Of home improvement grants; the drains
Have pleased the local drains inspector
Now human guests arrive by invitation
Made welcome at the shingled new front porch

The rabbits have gone, like Stobo, chased
Down a final burrow, stolen a last supper
Prepared by chemists and economists
A transistor emits a kind of music
The garden has been tamed and plotted
With basketweave fencing and privet hedges
Where the privy stood there's a child's climbing frame
From there on a clear day you can see gleaming
By the distant firth the nuclear reactor
Like a cartoonist's dream of a Martian city

In Defens

The City's brood of carrion creatures
Shrieked at their prey in ugly dissonance
And with hands clapped over ears
Applauding silence I broke clear

Leaving the day's paper crop
Of disasters unharvested without
The routine thanksgiving of pity
To seek lost woods and truant hills

To hear the dry conversation
Of conifers, and under some alders
A pool where trout fooled flies but not
Miraculous insects that Christlike

Criss-crossed untroubled waters
Indifferent to hosannas or doubt
Leaves above in the deep shadows twisted
Like knives in the wounds of the windless

Noon cool though a million stars
Blazed in a stream's chill furnace
And over fern-bearded boulders and
The shoulders of sheep-peppered hills

I heard the gutteral hinge of a grouse
Creak open the rusted gates of summer
Then pel-mel shadows of clouds like
Children running with clumsy kites

Poured headlong down the mitred valleys
Until an unseen aeroplane
Pregnant with Armageddon came
Pricking the blue baloon of the sky

Streaking its tautened skin with a white
Vaporous cut and all that summer
Landscape stopped its preening and snapped
Shut like a book that had lost all meaning

An Ambassador Is Recalled

(Fiat Justitia, Ruat coelum)

Black sky in Autumn
Trees creak in the wind
Folk roll like leaves
Along streets of the mind

Black cities crowd
On the back of the land
Like knots of veins
On an old man's hand

Young men run wild
And south fly the geese
In the diplomat's intray
Lie the remnants of peace

It the attache's portfolio
An epoch is burning
The harvest of history
Razed, to ashes turning

The slogans are deafening
Though children are calling
In the ambassador's brief case
The heavens are falling

QUANDARY

Random Memo

In reply to your missive of early September
When dawns leapt up like a flame I remember
And singed meridian clouds to vapour
The policy and resources committee paper
Is herewith returned, with all its platitudes

That blinding window flails like an overseer
In a slave ship bound for purple latitudes
This coal-heating system has burned since June
It will be hot as hell in here by noon
The bowels of the earth must be purged quite soon

That balcony girl thinks that nobody sees her
She removes a garment, flops on a chaise longue
Some kids chant a game in a demotic tongue
Hills waver above the blocked ventilator
I hear curlews yodelling from the radiator

I smell bog myrtle in its accordion haze
Your remarks anent strategy planning amaze,
Sphagnum feels cool on Cauldstaneslap
West in Glen Sannox a deer herd wrinkles
Old bracken, a stag on a crest bugles and bays

The wide blue highway of ocean twinkles
To the waiting world, the horizon a string
Of a silver clarsach poised for quivering
By a dauntless hand, likewise that girl
She removes her shoes. Children please stop

That chanting game before I drop
I want a song with percussive rigging
Pearling the foam awash in the gunnels
Throbbing to trade winds filling the sail
Ferrying me on to glittering isles

Caught like jade dragonflies in a web of light
Suspended in heat that flails with more pity
Than it does on this desk with its cargo of flies
But I only sail through appropriate channels
With the physical planning group steering committee

An ice vendor peels off a phrase by Strauss
She peels off something else, I think a blouse
Perhaps I'd waltz over if it weren't so warm
And attempt to complete her unofficial form
When all is removed with tender resignation

In response to the sun's latest notification
To all personnel on the staff of the world
Who have cast off moorings, whose sails are unfurled
Who don't have to write to the council member
In reply to his missive of early September

The Proper Sphere for Idealists

First a viscous rattling toy
Pink and filled with wondrous tricks
Then a thudding leather ball
Booted between a pair of sticks

Later a trembling idea others
Dropped deep into the night
Of themselves, that with years and journeys
Became a joy from which the sun gained light

Flagging but triumphant from
The welter and minatory throng
It was proffered whole and perfect
To one who had awaited both so long

Then tripping, it fell, was snatched
By another in the brawling street
Who transformed it to a gyve
And clamped it primly to his feet

The crowd thus cheated
Of the miraculous eclipse
Bore the temptress off chanting
Betrayal with cursing lips

Now when neighbours pass they say,
'She keeps it nicely polished though,
It really suits him don't you think?
He should have had one years ago.'

Wrong Cue

Everything had taken place
Exactly as directed until
That moment when you were meant
To emerge from French windows
Carrying the pruning clippers

To reach the rose you wanted
To wear with the new dress
For the premiere that evening
I had stepped up on the rain-tub
The view was clear over the walls

Traffic grumbled somewhere
But no-one seemed to be watching
Except for the audience: invisibly
Someone called 'Shears to grind'
If that is what was said

I couldn't remember the phrase
At rehearsals and turned to you
In surprise for explanation
You were almost at me by then
And you weren't holding clippers

As I fell twisting, the wound
Where the knife entered was long
This was not in the script
Likewise the hot rose-coloured flood —
What will the critics say

CONTINUUM

Exploring a Drawer when Young

Near brass handle-screws a glass
Souvenir paper-weight
Hold the hexagonal prism
To sunlight and rainbows leap
Across the Bridge of Sighs

Palm tractors over amber beads
Gale-dredged to Baltic shores
Carved and polished to rest
On the bust of a spinster aunt
Redolent of pot-pourri and lavender

Thimbles, confiscated catapults
Coloured marbles, cloudless worlds
Of wonder: embroidered antimacassars
Faded in the service of armchair-pounding
Elders setting their world to rights

Discarded briar of an older brother
Suck and puff at the mottled stem
Taste the ghost of stale smoke
And dust, remember long-inhaled
Fumes of bitter distrust

Probe deeper, disturb a nest of shells
A seaside holiday stirs from the debris
The clifftop sunset a burning peacock's tail
The mutter of the wind fretted
By a confetti of kittiwakes

Pebble in the last corner of all
Hungry breakers nibbling at the land
A lighthouse beam stampeding white horses
In the estuary, and someone calling —
A chandelier of stars lighting us home

Perpetuum Mobile

I walked past the house where I was born
There was no-one at home
But bulldozers had left visiting cards
And scaffolding for an execution
Across the debris of the lounge dandelions
Nodded with impudent grace in a breeze
Intent on plucking some fantails in the kitchen

A thrush was running over
A few cadensas in the music room

The last of the roof-ties grinned
An idiot's welcome above the remains
Of my bedroom ceiling through which
Long ago I had imagined
Constellations of the Great Teddy Bear
Golliwog Majoris and a pandrop odorous
Sunday school teacher of the first magnitude

Then a man entered from the kitchen garden
Where willow herb waved illicit blooms

A serious man with an organised sun
On his face and the future rolled under his arm
A neat white cylinder of the future
Enclosing its own principle of decay
And the promise of lorn gables
And a broken sky and a serious man
With a sunlit face and the future rolled under his arm

Tied up with an elastic band
Enclosing its own principle of decay
And the promise of lorn gables
And a broken sky and a serious man
With a sunlit face and the future
Rolled under his arm
A neat white cylinder of the future
Tied up with an elastic band
Enclosing its own principle of decay

And the promise

Elegy for Progress

(Written in Greyfriars Churchyard)

Stranger, I know that perplexity
I have leaned against the sunlight
To trace the Trajan-scripted epitaphs
Of merchants' wives and soldiers' children
Hearing flowers whisper over headstones
And seeing birds coil loops of song
Around forgotten sarcophagi

There is no room here for you, stranger
Your plot is required for a combine harvester
To reap an annual breakfast cereal
With bonus plastic toy for junior.
Under the azure brocade the ornate
Catafalque will sink in decorous time
To Handel's Largo beneath your kin

Then the real boxwood business
Will slide into a furnace, harder bones
Crushed, residual ashes of nerve and gut
Heart and sinew that sought the rarer light
In valued things, that burned with brighter
Love than those official flames
And strode Colossus-like among

The highest peaks and dared to scan
For better worlds — become as bitter
Dust blown from a flue, a wraith
Of soot to haunt a dreary suburb.
Better to know in that dwindling light
That birds would stir up lazy dawns
Behind the sculptured cypresses

And flowers stitch bright embroideries
Across a decent counterpane of turf
And better to know that a stranger might
Sometime pause to trace your span
And seemly epitaph and lean against
The sunlight and stare on the luminous heart
Of noon, but less perplexed than you

Interview

What happened then?
Well
Rush of
Guts bloody
Flux noisome matter
Cauls and wails ghouls
Caterwauls and shawls
All sprinkled with
Words and water
And there
I was

What happened then?
Well
Schools
With rules
Boots and balls
Bats and books pushing
Brats and boats fish
On hooks hills to
Climb and plenty
Of time
And there
I was

What happened then?
Well
Hair here
And there lots
Of spots crams and
Exams dreaming and streams
Rollcalls and jokes rams
And scrolls crowds of
Proud folks
And there
I was

What happened then?
Well
Wenching
And drenching
Testing protesting
An end to rugger toiling
And moiling hugger-mugger
Dread of treadmill will
To power seed sown
Strength grown to
Full flower
and there
I was

What happened then?
Well
Vague pains
Diminishing gains
Rheumy eyes stiff backs
Gaps in teeth and ranks
Dearest gone nearest going
Sparse thanks thrust aside
By once tiny hands park
Bands an end to
Sowing alone
And done bent
And spent
And there
I was

What happened then?
Well
Here
Lies

The Scarab

From a pellet of cattle excrement
Is born the image of an ornament
To adorn the breast of favoured
Odalisque or ancient empress

From the womb's agony is torn
A Helen, a Cleopatra is born
From ordure to glide by
Collonades of Troy or Karnak

The fumes and giant torments
Of a cooling world foments
A dream of Athens
Shadows of Rome lean forward

From dark ringed nebulae
Nascent suns endlessly
Shed planet sparks
As from blows on infinite anvils

Sparks that cool over aeons
To forest and hill, trembling oceans
By plains where forms
Are born of cattle grazing

Where insects trundle spheres of dung
From unknown beasts to house their young
Frail images of an ornament
Wrought by artistry impermanent

On gems unmined on planet Earth
To adorn our kin of stranger birth
Of other queens, another
Semiramis of a different Babylon

Where shepherds invoke an alien Spring
Where augurs praise God for everything

LIST OF SUBSCRIBERS TO THE SPECIAL EDITION

Elma F. Alexander, Edinburgh.

Bob and Melody Blyth, Shetland.

Richard G. Dewar, St. Ola, Orkney.

J. Gavin, Carlisle.

R. V. Gibson, Burlington, Ontario.

Malcolm Gilbertson, Kirkwall, Orkney.

Robin Harper, Edinburgh.

Paul Harris, Edinburgh.

Mrs. Johnnie Hughes, Hartlepool.

The Earl of Lauderdale, London.

Tom Leonard, Glasgow.

H. M. Murray Macrae, Edinburgh.

Morag MacGregor, Edinburgh.

Mary McGookin, Edinburgh.

Vera Peetz, Nottingham.

John Robertson, Edinburgh.

David and Alice Ross.

Phyl and Bill Scott.

Adrian Secchi, Edinburgh.

Charles Skilton, Edinburgh.

Mrs Hazel E. S. Smith.

Alasdair Steven, Strathtay.

Bill Tait, Shetland.

Paul Tibbald, Edinburgh.

John Watt, Milnathort.